Katy Kidd

and

The Long Scary Keyboard

Hidden Treasures Publishing
Katy Kidd and The Long Scary Keyboard
Text copyright © 2016 Jonnie Lee (Kidd) Whittington
Illustrations copyright © 2016 Bernice Adcock Talent
Cover creator: Jason Taylor
Editors: Patti Burman
        Ann Grisham

Summary: Katy has fun as she learns notes, rhythm, and gains other musical knowledge through a study of piano at school. By the end of the book she knows all of the keys on the piano, and can play a melody.

Library of Congress Cataloging-in-Publication Data
ISBN: 9781539699071
The Long Scary Keyboard
Jonnie Kidd Whittington
Bernice Adcock Talent – Illustrator
(Katy Kidd Series: book three)
1.Social skills 2. Finger co-ordination 3. Piano and music knowledge: rhythm, notes, counting, musical terms, finger exercise.
Printed in the United States of America

A note to parents from Jonnie Whittington

During my forty years of piano instruction, I have seen dozens of children's eyes grow large with fear when they tiptoed in for their first lesson.

"I don't know anything about this," they'd whisper.

I'd smile and say, "Good, I love to teach students who know nothing." I'd point. "This is a piano. Why don't you come over here and sit on the bench? We'll check it out." That put them at ease and from then on, they were fine.

I've taught students from age 4 to 74. They all learned.

Most thought their left hand was totally useless.

Many went from knowing absolutely nothing to playing for church. My own daughter and son are examples of this.

I felt it was time to share my knowledge with children everywhere.

This book is entertaining and informative. Your child will know the names of the 52 white keys on his/her completion and application of this first book with the Long Scary Keyboard.

Oh yes, I'm certified to teach through the St. Louis Institute of Music in Missouri.

My name is Jonnie Lee Kidd. You say it
Johnny, like a boy's name. I don't like that
so I'm changing it to a nickname - Katy.
That's right, just call me
Katy Kidd.

Chapter One

The Big Surprise

Monday - October 8, 1945

Today in school teacher has a secret surprise. With no warning, what-so-ever, she says, "A piano teacher will come to the school next week. If you want to take lessons, raise your hand."

My hand shoots up in the air. "I do, Teacher, I do," I yell. "Right here, Teacher. Me! Me! Me!"

"Yes, Katy, I see your hand."

Mrs. Jones walks calmly to my desk. "Take this note to your parents. It will explain about the lessons."

"I will, I will. This is a dream come true. I've wanted to learn piano for a really long time. Thank you, Teacher. Thank you!" I yell.

Teacher rubs her ear before she hands me the note. "You're welcome, Katy."

She smiles and turns to that cute boy Douglas. "Do you want one too?" she asks.

"Yes Ma'am," he says politely.

"Are you taking lessons too, Dougy?" I say. "Yea for you, 'cause I didn't know boys could learn that subject."

That boy nods his head and smiles. He shows his beautiful teeth except – uh oh! One of his best teeth is missing. With a hand on my hip, I ask that beautiful creature, "When did you become a snaggle-tooth, Dougy boy?"

He gives me a mean, frowny face. "None of your bees' wax, weighty Katy."

"I am not weighty I'll have you know. I am very skinny and thin as a rail. Thank you just the same, ugly Dugly."

"That's enough talking, Katy," teacher says very business-like. "We don't call people names in this class."

"Yes, Ma'am. But he called me one first. He called me weighty Katy, and you can see, Teacher, that I am not over weight at all. Therefore, he should not call me that bad name."

"I see that, Katy. Now, sit down and be quiet."

I do a little huff at that cute Douglas, who is not so cute anymore, and sit at my desk. All of my excitement about learning the piano is over. Now I probably cannot even learn to play that thing.

The next words Teacher says makes me forget all about that boy. She says, "The students who take piano lessons will leave class in the afternoon for fifteen minutes once a week. You will go down the hall to another room for your lessons."

"Will I go too, Teacher? Will I, huh?" I yell.

"Yes, you will if your parents give their permission and send the fifty cents to school for each lesson."

"That's all it costs?" I yell. "That's really good news. They can afford that, Teacher. I know they can give me fifty cents a week. Yes! This is a very good day after all." I turn to Douglas. "I am sorry," I say to that cute boy. "I will not call you ugly Dugly again, I promise."

He gives me a snaggle-tooth smile that makes me know he 'cepts my 'pology and says, "Thanks. I will not call you weighty Katy. I give you my word."

We are in agreedment. Now since that is cleared up, I can think of other things.

I can't wait to take home my note about piano lessons.

. . .

After school, I take the note in my hand and walk home with my sister, Bobbie.

"Lookee! Lookee!" I say and go through the door. I hold that note high in the air.

"A piano teacher is coming to our school. I can take lessons. It only costs the low price of fifty cents. Can I take 'em? Can I? Please!" I close my eyes, hold my breath, and wait.

"Let me read the note," Mama says. She takes it from my hand.

I cross my fingers and whisper on the inside, *Please.*

"I'll talk to your Daddy about this," Mama says and goes to the kitchen to cook supper. Daddy walks into the house. I run to him.

"Daddy, please can I take piano lessons? A teacher is coming during school hours. And guess what? It only costs fifty cents. Can we afford that, Daddy? Can we, huh?"

Daddy grins a big smile. "I believe we can afford that much, Katy. Yes, you can take them."

"Did you hear that, Mama?" I yell to her in the kitchen. "Daddy says I can take piano lessons. Isn't that the bestest news ever?"

"Yes, Katy," Mama hollers back. "Now wash your hands and come set the table for supper."

The most wonderful thing in my life is about to happen. Mama is not even jumping up and down about it. But I am!

Chapter Two

It's Almost Time

The big day arrives like any other day. My sisters, Norma and Bobbie and I get ready for school.

We eat bacon, fried eggs, grits and Mama's fluffy biscuits smeared with butter and jelly. That yummy stuff drips off my chin. I wipe it off with my fingers.

"Katy, wash your hands before you leave," Mama says. "Today's your first piano lesson. You don't want to get the keys all sticky with that guava jelly."

"Yes, Ma'am," I say very politely.

Mama and I take the dirty dishes to the sink. When I think about the lesson, scared flutters scurry around in my stomach.

My voice does a little gasp, "But Mama, I'm scared," I whisper.

She whirls around, "About what?"

"I don't know what to do at a piano lesson."

"Your teacher will tell you."

"But what if I don't understand?"

"Katy, other kids take lessons and they learn just fine. If they can do it - so can you."

Mama always tells me I can do things. I guess mamas are like that.

Thinking about it makes my heart go rat-a-tat in my chest. I want to put my hand on it to slow it down 'cept my palms are still sticky. And now they're sweaty too. I don't want to spoil my new red blouse.

"You do know, Katy, that you'll have to practice every day, don't you?"

I nod my head up and down and gulp. I'm not sure what she means by practice. If it means I have to sit real still for a long time, I don't want to do it.

"Now, don't worry, Katy." Mama smiles. "It won't be that hard. Your teacher will help you."

I nod again, but my heart says, rat-a-tat louder than before. "How many other kids will be there?"

"Five," Mama says and holds up all the fingers on one hand.

"Do I know 'em?"

"Yes, they are all in your classroom."

Whoever the other kids are, I bet right about now their palms are sweaty too. Maybe even their feet. I think they're scared as much as me.

Mama says, "If you like it, Katy, you can practice in the summer. That will keep you busy and you won't be bored."

Bored? What does that mean? Last summer I made mud pies, played jump rope, rode my bicycle, and played tag with my cousins. I didn't have time to be bored.

When music plays on the radio, I always bounce up and down 'cause I like music. Mama says that makes me a perfect candidate for piano playing.

Before I go out the door Mama says, "Give this money to Mrs. Jones first thing when you get to school." She gives me an envelope containing two quarters.

I hold it up, and see the outline of two circles. Keeping my fingers wrapped tightly

PIANO MONEY

around the envelope I make sure I don't drop the money.

At school, I walk into my classroom and go to Mrs. Jones' desk. "Here, Teacher, here is my piano money."

"Write your name on the envelope and I will put it in my drawer until time for your lesson. You must give the money to Mrs. McKenzie, the piano teacher."

"Is it time now? Where do I go?"

"No, not yet. You will go after lunch during our story time."

"Our story time! But I love story time. I don't want to miss that."

"I'm sorry, Katy, but that is when the teacher will be here. You will only miss fifteen minutes of the story on one day a week."

"Maybe I can live with that." I go to my desk. Now I have to wait for the piano lesson. Time crawls by . . . s l o w l y.

We do our numbers and our reading class. Then have recess before we practice writing our alphabet. Finally, we go to lunch.

When we have eaten, the teacher says, "Line up. It's time to go back to our class room." Excitement grips my stomach.

We march in a straight line. I swing my arms to keep up with the beating of my heart.

It's almost time!

Chapter Three

Finding the C's

Teacher takes out her story book. I love story time. Just as she opens the book, a woman walks into our room – a woman I've never seen before.

"Good afternoon, Mrs. McKenzie," Mrs. Jones says. "Class, this is the new piano teacher. Those who signed up for lessons, please stand and follow Mrs. McKenzie to the music room."

I stand and so does Douglas, Janie, Mary, Laura and Sam. I smile at Dougy. He turns his head away. My lips go in a straight line. I march with the others. Flutters start up in my belly.

We pass six doors before Mrs. McKenzie opens one and enters. Facing us on the other side is a big, tall piano. Excitement gathers in my eyes. I want to play that thing. I want to learn. I will. I will learn to play that piano.

"Boys and girls, please take a seat in the desks at the front of the class," Mrs. McKenzie says and taps Douglas on the shoulder. "You sit at the piano."

I stretch my eyes at that woman and raise my hand.

"Why does Dougy get to sit there?"

She smiles at me. "All of you will have a turn sitting at the piano. He's first today. Next week you will be first."

I smile at that woman.

"Raise your hand when I call your name," Mrs. McKenzie says. She comes to our desks and gives us a name tag. The one she pins on my red blouse says, KATY.

"This way I will know your name," she says with a smile.

I like her more and more.

On each of our desks she lays a keyboard made out of cardboard.

"Those sitting at a desk will pretend to play on these. I will watch your fingers to see if they are on the correct notes. I will listen to the person at the piano."

"Notice," she says, "there are black keys and white keys. The white ones are straight in a row like marching toy soldiers. The black keys are in bunches like bananas. Two to a bunch, and three to a bunch. With your right hand, touch and count the bunches that have two black keys."

"There's three on mine," I yell.

Teacher puts her finger to her lips and says softly, "Shhhh."

My hand goes down. My mouth shuts.

"How many are on the full piano, Douglas?" Teacher asks.

"Seven."

"Yes," she says. "Now class, count the groups that have three black keys."

"Three," I say softly.

"Yes." Teacher says. "Douglas, how many on the piano?"

"Seven."

"Correct." Teacher stops in front of my desk. "You can see that your desk keyboards are smaller than the full piano."

I nod my head.

"Now class, all of you come stand around the piano," Teacher says.

I hop right up. We gather in a group behind Douglas.

"Listen carefully," Teacher says. "See the name on the piano? It's just above the two black keys in the middle of the piano. The first letter of the name is where middle C lies."

"I see it!" I yell. "I see middle C."

"Douglas, with your thumb on your right hand play middle C," Mrs. McKenzie says.

That boy plays it ten jillion times.

"That's enough," Teacher says. "Now, go to the left and place your left hand at the end of the keyboard. Touch and play each C until you reach middle C."

Dougy boy nods his head and hits each note a little too hard, I believe.

"Change hands and let your right hand play the high C's until you play them all."

Douglas finds them going higher and higher. Bouncing his head up and down, up and down, he hits the notes too loud for my taste.

"Good. Now, stand up, Douglas, and let the other students take a turn to sit, find the C's and play them," Teacher says.

I quick sit down on the stool. I find them all.

"Did you see that, Teacher? I found all of them."

"Yes, I did, Katy. Now it's Mary's turn, then Janie's, Laura's and Sam's."

After we all play our C's, Teacher says, "For practice this week, find and play all of the C's on your own piano at home. Play them every day."

"Is that all, Teacher? Is that all we have to practice?"

"Yes, Katy, that's all." Mrs. McKenzie looks at the clock on the wall. "Class is dismissed. Line up and I'll escort you back to your room."

"That lesson was really fast, Teacher. It was easy too. I knew exactly what to do because you 'splained it real good."

"Explained is the correct pronunciation, Katy. And 'very well' not 'real good' is the correct grammar."

I smile at Teacher. "Yes, you EX-plained very well. Thank you," I say politely as I get in line in front of that cute boy, Douglas.

We head back to our room to what's left of story time.

Chapter Four

The Piano Practice Deal

My piano is waiting for me at home. After school, I walk through the door and see it sitting in the living room. My heart beats faster with excitement. I can't wait to find all of the C's on that thing.

I plop down on the bench. Right in front of my face is the name of the piano – Steinway.

"Hey, I never saw that before," I yell. "There it is. There is the S that begins the name of this thing. That is middle C."

I twirl around on that piano bench. "Bobbie, come here!" I yell.

Bobbie drops her books in the chair. "What do you want, Katy?"

I point. "Lookee, this is middle C, right here. Did you know that, Bobbie? Did you, huh?"

"No. How do you know, Katy?"

"Cuz that lovely piano teacher tells me, today, that's how. I like that lady. She is so nice and very smart."

"That's good, Katy."

"And look a here, Bobbie. Every place there are two black keys, the white key at the bottom is another C. That's exactly what the teacher says."

"So this is a C?" Bobbie points her finger and then she touches a key.

"Yes!" I yell. "You are exactly right. And this one and this one and this one." I yell pointing at all the C's one at a time. "I can't wait to learn the names of the other keys."

"When is your next lesson?" Bobbie asks.

I hang my head. My lips turn down. "Next Thursday," I whisper.

"I'm sorry, Katy, but you'll have to wait a whole week. You can keep finding the C's until then."

"Okay," I can barely hear my own voice.

"I have an idea," Bobbie says. "You can make up games. Start at the bottom of the keyboard and go up finding each C."

Bobbie continues, "Then start at the top where the high-sounding keys are and find them on the way down."

"That sounds like fun," I say and start the game. I'm done in a short time. "What other game can I play, Bobbie?"

Bobbie scratches her head and wrinkles up her face. "Hmm, let me think."

"I know one!" I yell. "I can count the C's and see how many are on the piano."

"Good," Bobbie says.

"One," I yell and put my finger on the lowest C. "Two," I say a little bit softer as I find the next one. "Three," is not as loud. "Four," is softer than before. When I reach the top C, I whisper, "Seven."

"That was fun!"

My big sister, Norma, passes by the piano. "There are eight, Katy. The top key is a C. Just because you can't see the two black keys doesn't mean it's not a C. It sits just above B.

"Oh," I say. "How did you know that, Norma?"

"Because I took lessons when I was a little kid like you."

"Then why don't you ever play?"

"Because I didn't like practicing. So my fingers didn't get the hang of it."

"Oh. Well, I will learn to play because I love to practice. That's what I'm doing now, and it's a lot of fun."

"I hope you do learn and keep on thinking it's fun. It *will* get harder, you know." Suddenly, Norma looks annoyed.

"Why am I wasting my time? I have to get my homework done so I can keep making A's." She leaves the room with her books in hand.

I turn back to Bobbie. "What else, Bobbie, huh? What else can I do?"

"Can you spread out your arms and reach both ends of the keyboard at the same time?" Bobbie asks.

I stretch out my arms. My fingers barely touch the bottom C and the top one. "Look, Bobbie, I can. I can reach them," I yell.

"Good. Now play one C with your left hand and then one with your right."

I stretch my left hand and look for the two black keys. Then I touch the lowest C. Next I reach my right hand to the top and find the C where the two black keys are missing. I play it.

"What's next Bobbie?"

"Bring your left hand up to the next C."

I come up and find it.

"Now your right comes down and finds the next one." Left-right, left-right, I continue until my hands finish.

I turn with a grin to Bobbie. "I did it! That was the funnest game of all."

"Good. That's your piano homework. Practice all those games every day and when you're older, you'll be a great piano player," Bobbie says.

"Wait, Katy, I have one more idea. I will get the stop watch and time you to see how long it takes to find all of the C's. At the end of the week, I'll time you again and see if you have gotten faster."

"It's a deal!" I yell. "I love that idea. You should be a piano teacher, Bobbie."

"Oh, I don't know, Katy. I don't know anything about it."

"I'll teach you what I learn every week, Bobbie, like I did today. And you can help me make up games for practice."

Bobbie sticks out her hand to shake. It is her time to say, "It's a deal."

Practice Lesson at home:

Find, play and count all of the C's on your keyboard.

Remember: they are the white keys to the left of the two black keys.

Chapter Five

The Happy Dog

After practicing my piano games every day, I grow tired of them. When I close my eyes, I can see all of the C's in my head. I am so ready for another lesson.

The next morning after breakfast, Mama says, "Don't forget your piano money today, Katy."

Excitement races through my body. "Today is Thursday?" I ask.

"Yes, it is. Today is your lesson."

"Yea! Hip, hip, hooray!" I yell. "I can't wait to learn another key."

"Don't lose your money," Mama says as she hands it to me on my way out the door.

I hold it tightly and write my name on the envelope as soon as I am at my desk. Then I give it to my teacher to keep until time for the lesson. Last week Laura lost her money and couldn't take her lesson. I do not want that to happen to me.

After the long morning, the piano teacher, Mrs. McKenzie, enters the room. Our regular teacher, Mrs. Jones, has just taken out the story book for the day. I want to hear her read. Disappointment rolls around in my stomach. My mouth swallows to make it stop.

Then I remember how much I long to learn the piano. Glad and happy I stand to my feet, ready to follow Mrs. McKenzie to the music room.

The other five piano students join us at the front of the room. We start our march down the hallway.

Once inside the music room, Mrs. McKenzie passes out the cardboard piano keys for our desks. We place them in front of us. All the C's stare me in the face.

"Who found all of the C keys on your piano this week?" Mrs. McKenzie asks.

"I did! Me! Me!" I yell. "I know all of them."

"Katy, you may go to the piano first."

"Thank you, Mrs. McKenzie," I say very politely. "I practiced them all week."

"Very good," she says. "Where is middle C?"

"I know that," I say softly. "It is right here. Right at the first letter of the name of the piano. You told us that last week and it is absolutely true."

"Very good, Katy. Now, show us all of the C's," Mrs. McKenzie says.

Very quickly I play each C on the whole keyboard. "Is that good, Teacher? Is it, huh?" I ask.

"Yes, indeed," she says. "Katy I can tell that you practiced this week. I'm proud of you. You may go back to your desk. Sam, come to the piano, please."

Sam takes his turn. Mrs. McKenzie gives each of us a chance to show that we know where to find all of the C's.

"Today we will learn the next key up from C," Mrs. McKenzie says.

My heart goes rat-a-tat in my chest 'cause I want to know, that's why. I lean up in my seat to hear every word.

"The key between the two black notes is D," Mrs. McKenzie says.

"Come class and gather around the piano. Each one will stand in front of a D. We will play it and say, "D is the dog with two black paws.""

We run to teacher. I am first to arrive. Each one of us finds a D. We see the two black notes and remember that is the dogs two paws.

We play D together and say the poem.

I can't wait to show Bobbie and tell her about the fun dog who turns over the ink. Then he walks through it. He climbs on the piano and leaves his black paw prints on the two black keys.

After school, as soon as we walk inside the house, I say, "You're going to love this next key, Bobbie. It is so cute."

"What is it, Katy?" she asks.

"The next one is D for Dog. Look it is right between the two black keys. They are the dog's paws. Can't you just see him sitting there on the white keys with his two paws on the black ones?"

"Yes I can imagine that, Katy."

"I'll stand at the highest D, Bobbie, and say, 'D is the dog with two black paws.' Now you run around me and play the next D and say the poem."

It's my turn to run around her and go to the D that is lower. I love saying the little rhyme.

When Bobbie plays the bottom D, I go to the top of the keyboard and start again. Then Bobbie goes to the top on the next round.

"We could do this all day, Katy," Bobbie says.

"Yes because it is the funnest game," I say.

We reach the top again and Bobbie plays the last D by herself. We stop.

"I like that game," I say, "and I already know where all of the D's are."

"You still have to practice them every day, Katy," Bobbie says.

"I know and I will practice the C's too."

"Let's time you on those and see if you are faster than when you played them last week," Bobbie says.

I run to find the stopwatch while she gets the pad of paper where she wrote the time last Thursday.

Sure enough I can play them faster than I did last week. *I sure do like piano practice. It's a lot of fun, and makes your playing sound better and better.*

Piano Practice at Home

Find all the D's on the piano. Say, "D is the Dog with two black paws."

Chapter Six

Cats, Dogs, and Elephants in a Zoo?

Thursday rolls around again; my stomach gets butterflies. I am so anxious to learn the next key on the piano.

When we walk down the hall, there are only three students this time. "Where are Mary, Sam and Laura? Why aren't those kids in here?" I ask.

"They are not taking lessons anymore," Mrs. McKenzie answers.

"What's wrong with them? Don't they like it?"

"They have their reasons."

"I don't want to quit. I love lessons about piano. Don't you Dougy and Janie? It's so much fun, huh?" I say and look at those kids. "I hope you don't stop too. 'Cause you can't learn if you quit."

"Let's begin our lesson," Mrs. McKenzie says. "The key we will talk about today is E. It is next door to the dog with two black paws. C is on one side and E is on the other side."

"I am so happy to know that," I say a little too loud.

We all get a chance to go to the piano and play all of the E's.

"Today I will teach you another way to remember the three keys you have learned," Mrs. McKenzie says. "Today we will pretend that the two black keys represent a zoo."

"How?" I ask. "How can it be a zoo?"

"Hold on, Katy, and I'll tell you," Mrs. McKenzie says with a little frown on her face. "There are three white keys around the two black keys. They are C, D, E. They represent three animals in the zoo. C means Cat, D stands for Dog and E is for Elephant."

"I like that!" I yell. "I like that a lot." I say a little quieter.

Mrs. McKenzie turns her frown into a smile. "Katy go to the piano," she says. "Show me all of the zoos on the piano and point out the three animals in each zoo."

I zoom out of my desk and fly to the front. I plop down on the bench and go to the left of the keyboard.

"Here's the first one," I say loudly so everyone can hear. "This is C, D, and E."

I play each key.

C D E

My finger finds the next two black keys. "That's another zoo," I yell. "another Cat, Dog and Elephant! I love this, teacher." I find all of the zoos and all of the C's, D's and E's.

"This is the bestest lesson of all," I say.

"Thank you, Katy." Mrs. McKenzie says. "You may go to your desk and find them on the cardboard keys. Janie come to the piano."

Douglas takes his turn next and then it is time to go back to our regular class.

We march down the hall. Back in the room, I am so excited about the lesson that it takes a while for me to listen during story time.

I finally turn my attention to Mrs. Jones. The story is about a poor family who moves to Florida.

They become dirt farmers or share croppers. I think that means they share the crop of food they plant. But I don't know who with. Teacher probably told the class while we were out of the room.

I feel sorry for the children in the story because they have to work really hard on the farm. They can't take piano lessons like me because they can't go to school.

They are happy to live in Florida where the sun shines every day. They pick strawberries in February while their cousins, who live up north, are freezing in the snow.

Though I love story time, this one makes me feel sad especially when the first crop fails. They don't have enough money to buy clothes for school. I like happy books; therefore, I am glad when story time is over.

. . .

At home, after school is out, I explain my new piano lesson to Bobbie and she finds all of the zoos and all of the C's, D's, and E's. Just like me, she loves this lesson.

I can't wait for next Thursday. What will I learn next? That's what I want to know.

Practice Lesson at home:

Find all of the Zoo's on your piano. Count them.

Find and play every C, D, E. You may want to call them Cat, Dog, and Elephant, but their real names are C, D, E.

Remember: they live on the three white keys closest to the two black keys that represent the Zoo.

Chapter Seven

The Crazy Music Garage

Mrs. Jones is reading more of the sad story the next week when Mrs. McKenzie comes to take us for our piano lesson. I am glad to go.

With only three of us in the class now, we each get to sit a little longer at the piano.

"Today is a big lesson." Mrs. McKenzie says. "Instead of one, we will learn two keys on the keyboard."

"What are they?" I ask politely.

"I knew you would ask, Katy," Mrs. McKenzie says with a smile. "Look at the keyboard on your desk."

Three heads bow at once to look.

"Do you see a set of three black keys?" she asks.

"Yes," I yell. "Yes, I do. In fact, I see three sets of them."

"Come to the piano, Katy, and count the sets of three black keys."

I bounce up to the front, smiling and happy to be first. Starting at the top, I count the sets of three black keys.

"Seven," I say. "There are seven sets of three just like there are seven sets of two black keys."

"That's correct, Katy," Mrs. McKenzie says. "We will pretend that the three black keys are a garage."

"With cars in it?" I ask.

"With two cars," Mrs. McKenzie says. "Right at the bottom of the garage next door to the E for elephant is F for Ford."

"My daddy had one of those. He had a Ford," I say softly. "But now he drives a Buick."

"Katy, you have just said the name of the next key we will learn. It is not next door to the Ford. It is at the top of the garage. You must skip two keys to find Buick."

"I found it," Dougy says.

Teacher checks to make sure he is on the correct key. "Very good, Douglas," she says.

I give that boy a frowny face. I wanted to find it first.

49

"It is right under the next C where the zoo is." I say very professional sounding.

"That's right, Katy," teacher says. "It is also below Middle C and every other C on the piano."

"And the next key after the last black key where there are three," I say.

"That's exactly right," teacher says softly.

We all have a turn to find the Fords which we know is really F and all of the Buicks for B. It's fun to name the keys animals and cars. Teacher is very smart to pretend the zoo and the garage.

With the lesson learned, Mrs. McKenzie walks us back to our class in time for more of Mrs. Jones' reading. Today, the sad story takes a happy turn. The crops thrive and the farmer makes enough money to buy the children new clothes. Now they can go to school.

I am so glad for them. I love going and learning. I don't want anybody to miss out on all the fun of school.

. . .

As soon as Bobbie and I arrive home, I am ready to show her the two new keys. She finds the Fords and the Buicks.

"Look, Katy," she says, "The Buicks are just below C."

"I know," I say. "We found that in class today. That's an easy way to remember 'em."

"There's only two keys left that you haven't learned yet, Katy." Bobbie says.

"Really?" I ask. "Only two?"

"Yes," Bobbie says. "Maybe your teacher will tell you both of them next week. Then you'll know all of the keys."

"I will?"

"Yes, you will."

I twirl around and do a little jig. "Only two more and I will know all of the keys!" I yell. "All of the keys on the whole piano!"

Mama comes into the living room. "What are you girls yelling about?"

"Next week I will know all of the keys on the piano." I say. Then I tell her each one's name that I already know.

"The two you don't know are G and A," Mama says.

My mouth flies open. "How do you know that, Mama?" I gasp.

"Because I took piano lessons. In the past I played the piano for church."

"You did?" I say with awe. "You know all of the keys?"

"Of course." Mama sits down, opens a hymn book and plays a song.

My mouth hangs open with surprise. "That sounds really, very pretty, Mama. I did not know that you could do that."

Mama smiles. "There's a lot you don't know yet, Katy, but you'll learn. I'm sure you'll learn."

What other surprises wait for me in this piano land? That's what I really, really want to know.

Practice Lesson at home:

Find and count all the bunches of three black keys on your keyboard.

Remember they are the garage with two cars.

Find each Ford. It is the first car in the garage and sits next to the Elephant. How many are there on your keyboard?

Now find each Buick. You will skip two notes and find Buick at the top of the three black notes. How many did you find?

Chapter Eight

Not a Baboon

I can't wait to tell Mrs. McKenzie that I already know the other two keys. Finally, Thursday comes. I grab my two quarters and put them in the envelope.

Instead of waiting until I'm at school to write my name on the envelope, I go to Daddy's office next to the dining room. A pencil is sitting right there in the cup. I grab it and write my name.

At school, I give it to Mrs. Jones. When the clock says it's time to go, Mrs. McKenzie comes into our room. I grab the money as Mrs. Jones hands it to me and out the door I hurry.

"Guess what?" I say to Mrs. McKenzie as we march down the hall.

"What is it, Katy?" she answers.

"I know a secret," I say real mysteriously.

"You do?" Mrs. McKenzie says. "What is your secret?"

"Can I whisper in your ear?" I say. "Cause I don't want that Dougy boy to hear."

She stops walking and bends down.

I speak into her ear. "I know the two new keys."

She gasps. "You do?"

"Yes." I whisper. "They are G and A."

"You are right." Her voice has disappointment ringing in it. Then her lips make a big smile. "But do you know their other names?" she asks.

"Other names? They have another name?"

"Yes, like the Ford and Buick. G and A have another name, too."

"Oh," I say. "I didn't think of that and my Mama didn't tell me either." Now I feel disappointment landing on my face.

When we are in the music room, teacher passes out our cardboard pianos. "Today I'm going to tell you the rest of the story."

"Story?" I say. "You will tell us a story?"

"The rest of the story I started last week. This is it. One day two animals ran away from the Zoo." She points to the two black notes on my keyboard. "They got between the two cars in the garage. Right between the Ford and the Buick."

Now she puts her fingers on the three black notes.

"This one," she says pointing to the G is an animal with a very long neck."

"A giraffe," Douglas says.

"How did you know that Dougy boy?" I say very politely but thinking that's not fair for him to know so fast.

Douglas shrugs his shoulders. "I just know these things."

Mrs. McKenzie says, "The next key is a big animal that lives in the jungle. It swings from the trees."

"Baboon," says Dougy.

"That's close, but it has another name."

Quick I think about Mama saying the key is an A. What animal starts with A and swings like a baboon?

"Ape," I yell just as soon as the word crosses my brain.

Correct," teacher says. I fold my arms and look down my nose at Dougy. *That should teach that boy a lesson. I know some*

answers, too. Even if I did have help from Mama.

We take turns going to the piano and finding the G's which are just above the F's, and the A's above the G's.

"Did anyone notice if you start two keys below Middle C the key is A? If you go to the right, you will play the first seven letters of the alphabet. A-B-C-D-E-F-G. Then it starts over."

"Oh! Yes, it does! I did not know that! Did you know that Dougy boy?" I ask very politely.

"I already saw it," he says through tight lips.

"Now that you know all of the keys on the piano, practice them this week," teacher says. "Next week we will learn to play a finger exercise.

I look at my fingers. Now my curiosity is really stirred up. What is a finger exercise? That's what I want to know.

Practice lesson at home:

Find and play all of the G's for Giraffe. Remember they are above the Ford and between the first two black notes in the bunches of three.

Now find all of the Apes for A. they are above the Giraffes between the two top black notes in a bunch of three and just below the Buicks.

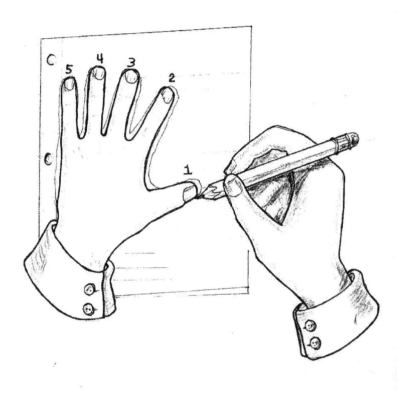

Chapter Nine

Thumbs are Big Guys

"Draw around your hand," the piano teacher, Mrs. McKenzie, says at our next lesson.

Douglas, Janie, and I lay our left hand on our piece of notebook paper with the blue lines. A pencil lays in the groove on the desk. I pick it up and do what teacher says.

"Here's mine, Teacher. See? Did I do a good job? Did I, huh? I drew around every finger."

"Yes, that's good, Katy."

"Why did we draw it?" I say. "That's what I would like to know."

"We are going to number our fingers," Mrs. McKenzie says. "Start with the big guy, the thumb. He is number one."

"He?" I yell. "My thumb is a he? How can that be? I'm a girl."

"Yes, Katy, we know that you're a girl. That is just a figure of speech," she says. "Write a one over your thumb on the paper."

I hurry and write the number 1. "Like this, Teacher? Is this right?" I hold up my paper so she can see it.

"Yes, that's right. Now, over your pointer finger write 2."

"We're going backwards. Aren't we, Teacher?"

"Yes, Katy, it appears that we are going backwards since that finger is to the left. In America we start reading on the left side of the page and go toward the right."

"Doesn't everybody read like that?" I say.

"No. In Israel they start on the right side of the page and read toward the left."

"Oh. Did you know that Dougy? Huh, did ya?"

I look at Douglas' picture. He draws around his right hand. "That is your wrong hand, Dougy," I say. "Your left hand is the one you do not write with."

"But I can write with either hand, smarty Katy," that Douglas says.

"No, you cannot. People are either left handed or right handed," I tell that mean boy. "Besides it is not nice to call me smarty Katy. Even though I am rather smart."

"Well, excuse me," he says, "but you are also wrong. Some people can write with either hand."

"That's correct, Douglas," says Mrs. McKenzie. "It's called ambidextrous."

"I did not know that," I whisper very softly. Embarrassment makes my face turn red.

"Class, finish numbering your fingers. When you are done, draw the other hand. Remember that each thumb is number one."

I hurry and try to beat that Dougy boy and Janie girl. I get my hand done fast. Uh oh, I make a big fat bubble on the side of one

65

finger. I quick go around again and erase where I got off base.

Douglas and Janie are both finished before me. I do a little huff and write the numbers.

"Hold your hands up," teacher says. "Not that high, Katy." I bring my hands down even with my face.

"That's better," she says. "Prop your elbows on your desk. That's good. Now wiggle your thumbs and say number one."

"Are we playing a game? Because if we are, I like it," I say.

"Yes, Katy. Now wiggle your pointers and say two."

We all do what teacher says, except I have to say, "Teacher, it's hard to do both hands at the same time."

"You may wiggle one finger at a time," teacher says. "Now wiggle your middle finger and call it three. Ring finger is four. Pinky is five."

When we finish, I ask teacher, "Is this the finger exercise, Teacher, is it?"

"No, Katy," she says. "Each of you make a cup in your right hand like this." Teacher rounds her fingers. "Now turn it over and keep your fingers bent. Place your thumb

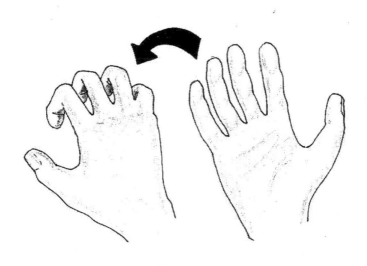

on middle C of your desk keyboard."

When I do that, my fingers go out straight. "Keep your fingers bent, Katy. You must play on the tips."

"That's hard, Teacher," I say.

"It is not hard for me," that smarty pants Douglas says.

I throw darts at him with my eyes. "Well, hooray for you, Dougy boy."

"That's enough, Katy," Teacher says from a frowny mouth.

I hang my head and say, very sweetly, "Yes Ma'am."

"You must keep your fingers bent so you do not damage them," teacher continues. "If you play incorrectly, it will make them turn up at the ends. I have seen teenagers whose fingers were very crooked from wrong playing."

"Did they stay like that forever?" I ask.

"Yes. Now children, make a cup, place your thumb on middle C then your second finger on D, your third finger on E, fourth finger on F and fifth finger on G. Play these one at a time like this." Teacher goes to the piano and plays.

"That was very pretty, Teacher. Didn't you like that, Janie?" I say.

Mrs. McKenzie says, "Now place your thumb on D and go up the scale with fingers one, two, three, four, five. Then put your thumb on E and again play fingers one, two, three, four, five going up to a different note each time."

I raise my hand.

"What is it, Katy?" Teacher asks.

"Is this the finger exercise?"

"Only half of it," she answers. "We will learn the other half next Thursday. Go to the piano, Katy," teacher says, "and play the half of the finger exercise we did today."

I swallow my spit 'cause I'm scared, that's why. I don't want to damage my fingers. I walk very slowly to the bench and sit. I make a cup and put my thumb on Middle C.

My fingers creep along on the keyboard very bendy. I don't want to have crooked fingers. I play on the tippy tips. One, two, three, four, five.

"That's good. Now move your thumb to D and repeat."

I keep moving my thumb up a note until I reach the next C. "Is that it, Teacher? Is that all?"

"No. You must do it with your left hand. Put your thumb of your other hand on Middle C and go down."

I do a little huff, 'cause I don't think my left hand wants to do that. I put it up there and I was right. My left hand is not co-operating.

"My left hand can't do this, Teacher. My left hand does not know how."

"It just needs more encouragement, Katy. Your left hand is very capable. It will do whatever you tell it to do."

"Really? It will?"

"Yes. You are in charge of your fingers. They do your bidding. Tell them what to do."

"Yes Ma'am." I tell my left hand to behave and do what I say, just the way Mama does me.

Guess what? My left hand plays the finger exercise very good. 'Cause I told it to, that's why. I am very excited to learn this good news.

Daddy always says, "You can do anything you put your mind to." Today my fingers learn that very important piece of information.

Practice lesson at home:

Place your hand on a piece of notebook paper. Draw around your hand. You may want to draw finger nails too. Number each finger.

Remember: thumbs are number one.

Now make a cup with your hand. Keep your fingers bent and place your right-hand thumb on middle C. Play each finger on the next note to play Katy's finger exercise.

Play one, two, three, four, five, on C, D, E, F, G. Now move your thumb up to D. Keep moving your thumb up and play 1,2,3,4,5. Keep moving your thumb up until it reaches the next C.

Remember to play it with your left hand. Place your thumb of your left hand on middle C. now, go down playing 1, 2, 3, 4, 5, on C, B, A, G, F. Move your thumb down to B and again play 1, 2, 3, 4, 5. Keep moving your thumb down and play 1, 2, 3, 4, 5, until your thumb reaches low C.

Chapter Ten

Count How Many?

"How many practiced your finger exercise this week?" Teacher askes us the next Thursday.

"Me, me! I did, Teacher!" I yell.

Dougy boy and Janie girl raise their hands quietly. What's wrong with them? Aren't they excited about this assignment? I love playing that beautiful piano. Bobbie timed me and my fingers got faster and faster.

"Wonderful," teacher says. "Today we will learn the second half."

"What is it, Teacher? Tell me. I really want to know," I say.

"I will give you a riddle - 'Everything that goes up must come down.' What do you think is the second half of the exercise?" Teacher says. "Remember, last week our right hand kept going up the keyboard."

Hum? I thought and thought. What could it be? Before my brain lands on the answer, that Douglas raises his hand.

"Do our fingers go up and then down?" he says.

"You're exactly right, Douglas," teacher says.

How did he know that? That is just not fair. I wanted to know it first.

"Go to the piano, Douglas, and play the full exercise," teacher says.

Now he gets to be first. That is really not fair.

Douglas plays one, two, three, four, five, and then he comes down. Five, four, three, two, one. He plays it very beautifully with his fingers all bendy. I want to play that good.

Each one of us gets a turn and teacher says, "You all did very well. Now today, we will learn about rhythm."

My eyes stretch big. That is something new. I love new stuff.

"Music is written on paper in the form of notes," teacher says. "Each note has a time value that determines how long your finger will sit on that key."

"How long, Teacher, how long will my finger sit on a key?"

That mean Douglas says, "You'll find out if you sit and listen, Chatterbox Katy,"

I fold my arms and do a double huff at that boy. "I am listening smart aleck Dougy."

"Be quiet, class," teacher says like she means it. "I cannot teach anything if you continue to talk."

I sit up straight and close my mouth. From the corner of my eye, I look at Dougy. He lifts his head and looks straight at Teacher.

"That's better," teacher says. "Now let's continue with the lesson on rhythm." She holds up a paper with a black Easter egg on it. A long stem grows out one side of the top and goes straight up.

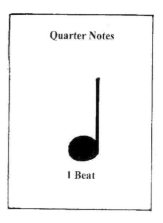

"This, class, is a quarter note. It is worth one beat," teacher says. "Janie, go to the piano and play a quarter note. Hold it long enough to say one, and then release it."

When she finishes, I raise my hand very politely.

"Yes, Katy," teacher says.

"May I play a quarter note too?" I ask.

"Thank you for raising your hand before you speak, Katy," teacher says, "but no, I want you to play a half note."

"I don't know a half note, Teacher, therefore I do not know how to play it," I say in my bestest voice.

Teacher, Mrs. McKenzie, holds up another picture of a note. It is a white egg and has a stem growing out the top. "This is a half note, class. It is worth two beats."

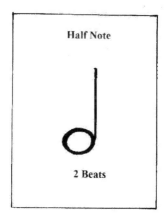

I raise my hand and say, "Oh, oh, Teacher. Does that mean I will play the note and say one, two? Does it teacher? Is that how I play a half note?"

"Yes, Katy. Go to the piano. Janie stay there. Katy play any high note and count - one, two."

I do exactly what Teacher says. "Was that right, Teacher? Was that a half note? Was it, huh?"

"Yes, Katy. Now Douglas go to the bass side of the piano and play a whole note." She holds up a picture of a round circle that looks like a donut.

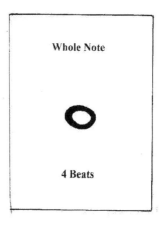

Whole Note

4 Beats

"This is a whole note. It is worth four beats," she says.

Douglas steps to the left of Janie and plays a low growly note and counts one, two, three, four in a deep voice.

"That's correct, Douglas."

Teacher holds up a picture of two black notes with a bar connecting them together at the top of the stems. All of you will play the next two notes.

"These notes are eighth notes. I like to call them 'play fast' notes. They each get half a beat. It takes both of them together to make one beat."

Teacher plays them very fast and says, "Play fast."

"Now each of you play the eighth notes by yourself. Remember they go twice as fast as a quarter note."

Each of us take a turn playing the two fast notes. "That's fun," I say. "I like the fast notes the best."

"Well and good, Katy, but it takes all of the notes to play a pretty song," teacher says.

"We have one more note." Teacher holds up a half note with a dot beside it. "The name of this one is easy. It is a half note with a dot beside it. Its name is dotted half note."

The half note gets two beats but the dot adds half as much, which is one. Two plus one is three. The dotted half note is worth three beats.

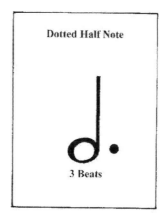

Dotted Half Note

3 Beats

Next, teacher does a little game where she calls out the kind of note she wants us to play. She holds up the picture and says its name. We have to remember how many beats to hold it.

We play together. "I remember the beats for each one of them," I say rather loudly.

"You're not the only one, Katy," says that Douglas. "I know them, too."

"Me, too," whispers that quiet girl, Janie.

"Each of you did very well. Next week we will learn to play a song."

Excitement leaps inside me. I want to jump up and down. Instead, I follow teacher back to our regular classroom.

I can't wait until school is out so I can draw pictures of the notes and tell Bobbie all about them. She can play them for their proper amount of time.

Then I'll tell her, "Bobbie, guess what? Next week we will learn how to play a song. A real song. Isn't that good?"

And Bobbie will say, "That's very good, Katy. I can't wait to learn it."

And I'll say, "I can't wait either."

Will next Thursday ever come?

Practice lesson at home:

1. Learn the value for the notes

Quarter note = 1 beat

Half note = 2 beats

Dotted half note = 3 beats

Whole note = 4 beats

Eighth notes = ½ beat each or it takes two to make one beat. We call them play fast.

2. Play the full finger exercise: 1, 2, 3, 4, 5, 4, 3, 2, 1 on C, D, E, F, G, F, E, D, C. Then put your thumb on D and play it again 123454321. Keep moving up until your thumb reaches high C.

Don't forget to play it with your left hand. Place your thumb on middle C and go down. Play 123454321. Move your thumb down to B and play again 123454321. Keep moving down until your thumb reaches low C.

Chapter Eleven

Not So Golden

"Class, today, we will learn a song with the three notes from last week," piano teacher, Mrs. McKenzie says. "It has words so you may sing after you have learned to play the notes."

I raise my hand, very politely.

"Yes, Katy," teacher says.

"May I be first?" I say and look at that boy Douglas from the corner of my eye.

"Since you were so polite, you may be first. Go to the piano," Teacher says very sweetly. "However," she continues, "in the future you may want to think of others ahead of yourself. Do you know the golden rule?"

I look up and down and shake my head side to side. "No Ma'am." I think some more and say, "I *do* know that gold is very shiny and pretty. I do *not* know the golden rule?"

"Do unto others as you would have them do unto you," teacher says.

"Hum." I scratch my head and think about her words. *What do they mean?*

"Does that mean I should let Janie, or Douglas be first because I want them to let me be first?" I say in a whisper.

"Yes, that is exactly what it means," she says.

I look at that boy Douglas and that girl Janie. I do not like this rule. It is not shiny or pretty like gold. "Why, teacher? Why should I let them go first?"

"Because God has a law. It says that the good we do for others will come back to bless us," teacher says.

"Hum." I want to be blessed . . . but I do not want to do the golden rule . . . Should I try it? "Okay, teacher. I will do it. I will let Janie go first."

"That's very kind of you, Katy," teacher says. "Janie, go to the piano."

That girl sits on the bench. Teacher gives each one of us a paper with the names of the notes on it. This is what I see:

C C C C D D D D. E E E E
1 1 1 1 1 1 1 1 1 1 1 1
I just love to play pi - an - o.   I just love to

D D D D.
1 1 1 1
play pi - an - o.

C C C C D D D D E D C
1 1 1 1 1 1 1 1 1-2 1-2 1234
I just love to play pi - an–o . Play and sing

"First, class, we will play and say the name of each note."

We do just as teacher says. It is a little bit hard to do. I am happy to play on my cardboard piano so no one can hear it. Now I'm glad I let Janie go first. This golden rule really works.

Teacher says, "Second, we will play again and say the number under the note.

That is the value or how long we hold that note. Most of them are quarter notes. How many beats does a quarter note get?"

All three of us raise our hand.

"All of you tell me together," teacher smiles and says.

"ONE," we all shout in unison. That word means we say it at the same time.

"Correct," teacher says. "Look at the end of the song. Do you see that we have two half notes and one whole note?"

"Yes," we say more quietly.

"And how many beats does a half note get?"

"Two," we say together.

"And a whole note is worth how much?"

"Four." I hold up four fingers. I look at Douglas and Janie. They each have four fingers in the air, too.

"Class, I can see that you have been practicing your note values. That makes me very proud of you. Thank you."

"Are you proud of me, too?" I ask very sweetly.

"Yes, Katy I am very proud of you for practicing the piano and keeping the golden rule."

"Now, class," teacher says, "we will play our song once more and this time we will sing the words."

It was very hard to play the note and sing the words at the same time. I will practice every day. I want to play. I want to sing.

"Today is our last lesson until after the Christmas holidays," Teacher says.

"Oh no," I groan.

"What is it, Katy?" teacher says.

"I will miss my piano lessons."

Teacher smiles and says, "But you'll enjoy the gifts under the tree."

Thinking about presents makes me feel good. I do a little happy dance.

After Christmas I will learn a lot more stuff about the piano. I will teach it all to Bobbie.

I'm glad Christmas is coming, but I can't wait to get back to my favorite thing - piano lessons.

Practice lesson at home:

Play the song on page 86 that Katy learned. Play it three times like this:

1. *Play and say the names of the notes.*
2. *Play and count the beats.*
3. *Play and sing the words.*

Words that Katy uses incorrectly

Incorrect	Correct
Agreedment	Agreement
Bestest	Best
Quick	Quickly
'Splained	Explained
Real good	Very well
'Cause	Because
Funnest	Most fun
Askes	Asks

Katy is using fewer words incorrectly as she grows and learns in school.

Dear Reader:

CONGRATULATIONS! You know all of the keys on your piano, and you can play a song.

Remember that Katy has:

Coloring Book Three to match this reader.

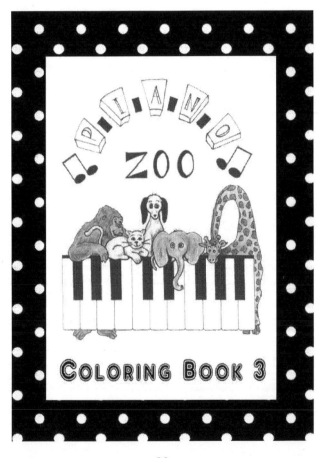

I can't wait for you to see the fun Katy has and what she learns in the next book called:

Katy Kidd and the

Not So Scary Keyboard.

Will she learn to read the notes on music paper? You can learn that, too. Will she learn to play a song with a chord? That will be so exciting if she does! You can learn it with her!

The next book will be out soon!

It is called:

Katy Kidd and the

Not So Scary Keyboard

by

Jonnie Kidd Whittington

Illustrated by

Bernice Adcock Talent

Your mother can order it at amazon.com.

Happy reading and piano playing!

Made in the USA
Columbia, SC
01 December 2024

47357504R00057